THE WAY OF THE

BUDDHA

THE WAY OF THE

BUDDHA

TRANSLATED FROM PALI BY F. MAX MÜLLER

with illustrations from the Rubin Museum of Art

ABRAMS, NEW YORK

CONTENTS

CHAPTER I: The Twin-Verses 7

CHAPTER II: On Earnestness 21

CHAPTER III: Thought 31

CHAPTER IV: Flowers 39

CHAPTER V: The Fool 49

CHAPTER VI: The Wise Man (Pandita) 61

CHAPTER VII: The Venerable (Arhat) 71

CHAPTER VIII: The Thousands 79

CHAPTER IX: Evil 89

CHAPTER X: Punishment 97

CHAPTER XI: Old Age 109

CHAPTER XII: Self 117

CHAPTER XIII: The World. 125

CHAPTER XIV: The Buddha (The Awakened) 135

CHAPTER XV: Happiness. 147

CHAPTER XVI: Pleasure. 157

CHAPTER XVII: Anger 165

CHAPTER XVIII: Impurity 175

CHAPTER IXX: The Just 191

CHAPTER XX: The Way 201

CHAPTER XXI: Miscellaneous 213

CHAPTER XXII: The Downward Course 225

CHAPTER XXIII: The Elephant 237

CHAPTER XXIV: Thirst 249

CHAPTER XXV: The Bhikshu (Mendicant) 267

CHAPTER XXVI: The Brahmana (Arhat) 285

LIST OF ILLUSTRATIONS 310

CHAPTER I

THE TWIN-VERSES

1

All that we are is the result of what we have thought: it is founded on our thoughts, it is made up of our thoughts. If a man speaks or acts with an evil thought, pain follows him, as the wheel follows the foot of the ox that draws the carriage.

2

All that we are is the result of what we have thought: it is founded on our thoughts, it is made up of our thoughts. If a man speaks or acts with a pure thought, happiness follows him, like a shadow that never leaves him.

"He abused me, he beat me, he defeated me, he robbed me"—in those who harbor such thoughts hatred will never cease.

"He abused me, he beat me, he defeated me, he robbed me"—in those who do not harbor such thoughts hatred will cease.

For hatred does not cease by hatred at any time: hatred ceases by love—this is an old rule.

The world does not know that we must all come to an end here; but those who know it, their quarrels cease at once.

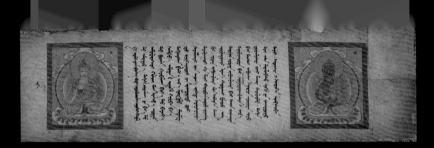

7

He who lives looking for pleasures only, his senses uncontrolled, immoderate in his food, idle, and weak, Mâra (the tempter) will certainly overthrow him, as the wind throws down a weak tree.

8

He who lives without looking for pleasures, his senses well controlled, moderate in his food, faithful and strong, him Mâra will certainly not overthrow, any more than the wind throws down a rocky mountain.

He who wishes to put on the yellow dress without having cleansed himself from sin, who disregards temperance and truth, is unworthy of the yellow dress.

But he who has cleansed himself from sin, is well grounded in all virtues, and endowed also temperance and truth, he is indeed worthy of the yellow dress.

They who imagine truth in untruth, and see untruth in truth, never arrive at truth, but follow vain desires.

They who know truth in truth, and untruth in untruth, arrive at truth, and follow true desires.

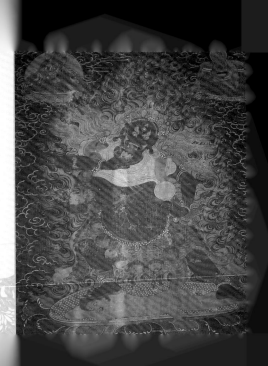

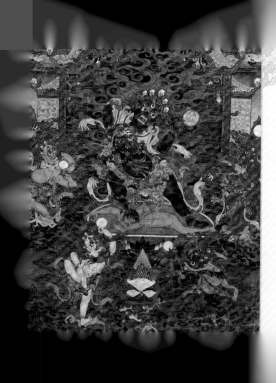

As rain breaks through an ill-thatched house, passion will break through an unreflecting mind.

As rain does not break through a well-thatched house, passion will not break through a well-reflecting mind.

15

The evildoer mourns in this world, and he mourns in the next; he mourns in both. He mourns and suffers when he sees the evil of his own work.

16

The virtuous man delights in this world, and he delights in the next; he delights in both. He delights and rejoices, when he sees the purity of his own work.

The evildoer suffers in this world, and he suffers in the next; he suffers in both. He suffers when he thinks of the evil he has done; he suffers more when going on the evil path.

The virtuous man is happy in this world, and he is happy in the next; he is happy in both. He is happy when he thinks of the good he has done; he is still more happy when going on the good path.

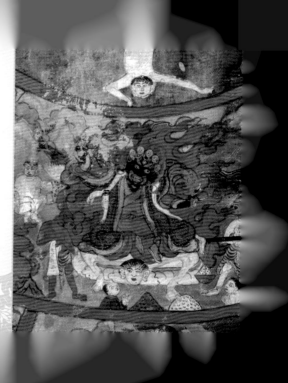

The thoughtless man, even if he can recite a large portion (of the law), but is not a doer of it, has no share in the priesthood, but is like a cowherd counting the cows of others.

The follower of the law, even if he can recite only a small portion (of the law), but, having forsaken passion and hatred and foolishness, possesses true knowledge and serenity of mind, he, caring for nothing in this world or that to come, has indeed a share in the priesthood.

ON
EARNESTNESS

Earnestness is the path of immortality (Nirvâna), thoughtlessness the path of death. Those who are in earnest do not die, those who are thoughtless are as if dead already.

Having understood this clearly, those who are advanced in earnestness delight in earnestness, and rejoice in the knowledge of the elect.

These wise people, meditative, steady, always possessed of strong powers, attain to Nirvana, the highest happiness.

If an earnest person has roused himself, if he is not forgetful, if his deeds are pure, if he acts with consideration, if he restrains himself, and lives according to law—then his glory will increase.

By rousing himself, by earnestness, by restraint and control, the wise man may make for himself an island which no flood can overwhelm.

Fools follow after vanity. The wise man keeps earnestness as his best jewel.

Follow not after vanity, nor after the enjoyment of love and lust! He who is earnest and meditative, obtains ample joy.

When the learned man drives away vanity by earnestness, he, the wise, climbing the terraced heights of wisdom, looks down upon the fools: free from sorrow he looks down upon the sorrowing crowd, as one that stands on a mountain looks down upon them that stand upon the plain.

Earnest among the thoughtless, awake among the sleepers, the wise man advances like a racer, leaving behind the hack.

By earnestness did Maghavan (Indra) rise to the lordship of the gods. People praise earnestness; thoughtlessness is always blamed.

A Bhikshu (mendicant) who delights in earnestness, who looks with fear on thoughtlessness, moves about like fire, burning all his fetters, small or large.

A Bhikshu (mendicant) who delights in reflection, who looks with fear on thoughtlessness, cannot fall away from his perfect state—he is close upon Nirvâna.

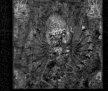

CHAPTER III

THOUGHT

As a fletcher makes straight his arrow, a wise man makes straight his trembling and unsteady thought, which is difficult to guard, difficult to hold back.

As a fish taken from his watery home and thrown on dry ground, our thought trembles all over in order to escape the dominion of Mâra, the tempter.

It is good to tame the mind, which is difficult to hold in and flighty, rushing wherever it listeth; a tamed mind brings happiness.

Let the wise man guard his thoughts, for they are difficult to perceive, very artful, and they rush wherever they list: thoughts well guarded bring happiness.

Those who bridle their mind which travels far, moves about alone, is without a body, and hides in the chamber of the heart, will be free from the bonds of Mâra, the tempter.

If a man's faith is unsteady, if he does not know the true law, if his peace of mind is troubled, his knowledge will never be perfect.

If a man's thoughts are not dissipated, if his mind is not perplexed, if he has ceased to think of good or evil, then there is no fear for him while he is watchful.

Knowing that this body is fragile like a jar, and making this thought firm like a fortress, one should attack Mâra, the tempter, with the weapon of knowledge, one should watch him when conquered, and should never rest.

Before long, alas! this body will lie on the earth, despised, without understanding, like a useless log.

42

Whatever a hater may do to a hater, or an enemy to an enemy, a wrongly directed mind will do us greater mischief.

43

Not a mother, not a father, will do so much, nor any other relatives; a well-directed mind will do us greater service.

CHAPTER IV

FLOWERS

Who shall overcome this earth, and the world of Yama the lord of the departed, and the world of the gods? Who shall find out the plainly shown path of virtue, as a clever man finds out the right flower?

The disciple will overcome the earth, and the world of Yama, and the world of the gods. The disciple will find out the plainly shown path of virtue, as a clever man finds the right flower.

He who knows that this body is like froth, and has learned that it is as unsubstantial as a mirage, will break the flower-pointed arrow of Mâra, and never see the king of death.

Death carries off a man who is gathering
flowers, and whose mind is distracted,
as a flood carries off a sleeping village.

Death subdues a man who is gathering
flowers, and whose mind is distracted,
before he is satiated in his pleasures.

As the bee collects nectar and departs without injuring the flower, or its color or scent, so let a sage dwell in his village.

Not the perversities of others, not their sins of commission or omission, but his own misdeeds and negligences should a sage take notice of.

Like a beautiful flower, full of color, but without scent, are the fine but fruitless words of him who does not act accordingly.

But, like a beautiful flower, full of color and full of scent, are the fine and fruitful words of him who acts accordingly.

As many kinds of wreaths can be made from a heap of flowers, so many good things may be achieved by a mortal when once he is born.

The scent of flowers does not travel against the wind, nor that of sandalwood, or of Tagara and Mallikâ flowers; but the odor of good people travels even against the wind; a good man pervades every place.

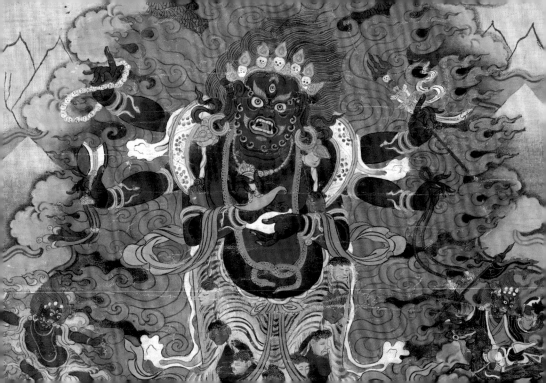

Sandalwood or Tagara, a lotus-flower, or a Vassiki, among these sorts of perfumes, the perfume of virtue is unsurpassed.

Mean is the scent that comes from Tagara and sandalwood; the perfume of those who possess virtue rises up to the gods as the highest.

Of the people who possess these virtues, who live without thoughtlessness, and who are emancipated through true knowledge, Mâra, the tempter, never finds the way.

As on a heap of rubbish cast upon the highway the lily will grow full of sweet perfume and delight, thus among those who are mere rubbish the disciple of the truly enlightened Buddha shines forth by his knowledge above the blinded worldling.

CHAPTER V

THE
FOOL

Long is the night to him who is awake;
long is a mile to him who is tired; long
is life to the foolish who do not know
the true law.

If a traveler does not meet with one who
is his better, or his equal, let him firmly
keep to his solitary journey; there is no
companionship with a fool.

"These sons belong to me, and this wealth belongs to me," with such thoughts a fool is tormented. He himself does not belong to himself; how much less sons and wealth?

The fool who knows his foolishness, is wise at least so far. But a fool who thinks himself wise, he is called a fool indeed.

64

If a fool be associated with a wise man even all his life, he will perceive the truth as little as a spoon perceives the taste of soup.

65

If an intelligent man be associated for one minute only with a wise man, he will soon perceive the truth, as the tongue perceives the taste of soup.

Fools of poor understanding have themselves for their greatest enemies, for they do evil deeds which must bear bitter fruits.

That deed is not well done of which a man must repent, and the reward of which he receives crying and with a tearful face.

No, that deed is well done of which a man does not repent, and the reward of which he receives gladly and cheerfully.

As long as the evil deed done does not bear fruit, the fool thinks it is like honey; but when it ripens, then the fool suffers grief.

Let a fool month after month eat his food (like an ascetic) with the tip of a blade of Kuśa's grass, yet he is not worth the sixteenth particle of those who have well weighed the law.

An evil deed, like newly drawn milk, does not turn suddenly; smoldering, like fire covered by ashes, it follows the fool.

And when the evil deed, after it has become known, brings sorrow to the fool, then it destroys his bright lot, nay, it cleaves his head.

Let the fool wish for a false reputation, for precedence among the Bhikshus, for lordship in the convents, for worship among other people!

"May both the layman and he who has left the world think that this is done by me; may they be subject to me in everything which is to be done or is not to be done," thus is the mind of the fool, and his desire and pride increase.

"One is the road that leads to wealth, another the road that leads to Nirvâna;" if the Bhikshu, the disciple of Buddha, has learned this, he will not yearn for honor, he will strive after separation from the world.

THE
WISE MAN (PANDITA)

If you see a man who tells you what is to be avoided, who administers reproofs, and is intelligent, follow that wise man as you would one who tells of hidden treasure; it will be better, not worse, for him who follows him.

Let him admonish, let him teach, let him forbid what is improper!—he will be beloved of the good, by the bad he will be hated.

Do not have evildoers for friends, do not have low people for friends: have virtuous people for friends, have for friends the best of men.

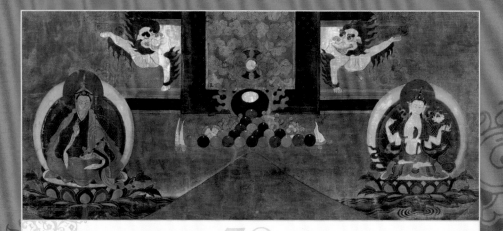

He who drinks in the law lives happily with a serene mind: the sage rejoices always in the law, as preached by the elect.

Well-makers 80 lead the water wherever they like; fletchers bend the arrow; carpenters bend a log of wood; wise people fashion themselves.

As a solid rock 81 is not shaken by the wind, wise people falter not amidst blame and praise.

Wise people, after 82 they have listened to the laws, become serene, like a deep, smooth, and still lake.

Good men indeed walk warily under all circumstances; good men speak not out of desire for sensual gratification; whether touched by happiness or sorrow wise people never appear elated or depressed.

If, whether for his own sake, or for the sake of others, a man wishes neither for a son, nor for wealth, nor for lordship, and if he does not wish for his own success by unfair means, then he is good, wise, and virtuous.

Few are there among men who arrive at the other shore become Arhats; the other people here run up and down the shore.

But those who, when the law has been well preached to them, follow the law, will pass over the dominion of death, however difficult to cross.

A wise man should leave the dark state of ordinary life, and follow the bright state of the Bhikshu. After going from his home to a homeless state, he should in his retirement look for enjoyment where enjoyment seemed difficult. Leaving all pleasures behind, and calling nothing his own, the wise man should purge himself from all the troubles of the mind.

Those whose mind is well grounded in the seven elements of knowledge, who without clinging to anything, rejoice in freedom from attachment, whose appetites have been conquered, and who are full of light, are free even in this world.

CHAPTER VII

THE
VENERABLE (ARHAT)

There is no suffering for him who has finished his journey, and abandoned grief, who has freed himself on all sides, and thrown off all fetters.

They exert themselves with their thoughts well collected, they do not tarry in their abode; like swans who have left their lake, they leave their house and home.

Men who have no riches, who live on recognized food, who have perceived void and unconditioned freedom (Nirvâna), their path is difficult to understand, like that of birds in the air.

He whose appetites are stilled, who is not absorbed in enjoyment, who has perceived void and unconditioned freedom (Nirvâna), his path is difficult to understand, like that of birds in the air.

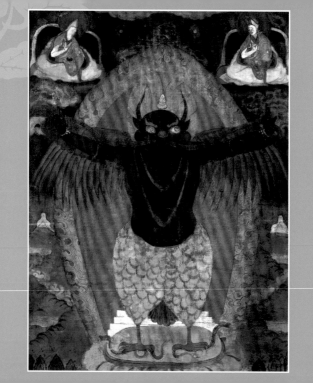

The gods even envy him whose senses, like horses well broken in by the driver, have been subdued, who is free from pride, and free from appetites; such a one who does his duty is tolerant like the earth, or like a threshold; he is like a lake without mud; no new births are in store for him.

His thought is quiet, quiet are his word and deed, when he has obtained freedom by true knowledge, when he has thus become a quiet man.

The man who is free from credulity, but knows the uncreated, who has cut all ties, removed all temptations, renounced all desires, he is the greatest of men.

In a hamlet or in a forest, in the deep water or on the dry land, wherever venerable persons (Arhanta) dwell, that place is delightful.

Forests are delightful; where the world finds no delight, there the passionless will find delight, for they look not for pleasures.

CHAPTER VIII

THE
THOUSANDS

Even though a speech be a thousand (of words), but made up of senseless words, one word of sense is better, which if a man hears, he becomes quiet.

Even though a Gâthâ (poem) be a thousand (of words), but made up of senseless words, one word of a Gâthâ is better, which if a man hears, he becomes quiet.

Though a man recite a hundred Gâthâs made up of senseless words, one word of the law is better, which if a man hears, he becomes quiet.

If one man conquer in battle a thousand times a thousand men, and if another conquer himself, he is the greatest of conquerors.

One's own self conquered is better than all other people; not even a god, a Gandharva, not Mâra (with Bráhman) could change into defeat the victory of a man who has vanquished himself, and always lives under restraint.

If a man for a hundred years sacrifice month after month with a thousand, and if he but for one moment pay homage to a man whose soul is grounded in true knowledge, better is that homage than sacrifice for a hundred years.

If a man for a hundred years worship Agni (fire) in the forest, and if he but for one moment pay homage to a man whose soul is grounded in true knowledge, better is that homage than sacrifice for a hundred years.

Whatever a man sacrifice in this world as an offering or as an oblation for a whole year in order to gain merit, the whole of it is not worth a quarter a farthing; reverence shown to the righteous is better.

He who always greets and constantly reveres the aged, four things will increase to him: life, beauty, happiness, power.

But he who lives a hundred years, vicious and unrestrained, a life of one day is better if a man is virtuous and reflecting.

And he who lives a hundred years, ignorant and unrestrained, a life of one day is better if a man is wise and reflecting.

And he who lives a hundred years, idle and weak, a life of one day is better if a man has attained firm strength.

And he who lives a hundred years, not seeing beginning and end, a life of one day is better if a man sees beginning and end.

And he who lives a hundred years, not seeing the immortal place, a life of one day is better if a man sees the immortal place.

And he who lives a hundred years, not seeing the highest law, a life of one day is better if a man sees the highest law.

CHAPTER IX

EVIL

A man should hasten towards the good, he should keep his thought away from evil; if a man does what is good slothfully, his mind delights in evil.

If a man commits a sin, let him not do it again; let him not delight in sin: the accumulation of evil is painful.

If a man does what is good, let him do it again; let him delight in it: the accumulation of good is delightful.

Even an evildoer sees happiness so long as his evil deed does not ripen; but when his evil deed ripens, then does the evildoer see evil.

Even a good man sees evil days, so long as his good deed does not ripen; but when his good deed ripens, then does the good man see good things.

Let no man think lightly of evil, saying in his heart, It will not come nigh unto me. Even by the falling of water-drops a water-pot is filled; the fool becomes full of evil, even if he gather it little by little.

Let no man think lightly of good, saying in his heart, It will not come nigh unto me. Even by the falling of water-drops a water-pot is filled; the wise man becomes full of good, even if he gather it little by little.

Let a man avoid evil deeds, as a merchant, if he has few companions and carries much wealth, avoids a dangerous road; as a man who loves life avoids poison.

He who has no wound on his hand, may touch poison with his hand; poison does not affect one who has no wound; nor is there evil for one who does not commit evil.

If a man offend a harmless, pure, and innocent person, the evil falls back upon that fool, like light dust thrown up against the wind.

Some people are born again; evildoers go to hell; righteous people go to heaven; those who are free from all worldly desires attain Nirvâna.

Not in the sky, not in the midst of the sea, not if we enter into the clefts of the mountains, is there known a spot in the whole world where a man might be freed from an evil deed.

Not in the sky, not in the midst of the sea, not if we enter into the clefts of the mountains, is there known a spot in the whole world where death could not overcome the mortal.

CHAPTER X

PUNISHMENT

129

All men tremble at punishment, all men fear death; remember that you are like unto them, and do not kill, nor cause slaughter.

130

All men tremble at punishment, all men love life; remember that thou art like unto them, and do not kill, nor cause slaughter.

He who, seeking his own happiness, punishes or kills beings who also long for happiness, will not find happiness after death.

He who, seeking his own happiness, does not punish or kill beings who also long for happiness, will find happiness after death.

Do not speak harshly to anybody; those who are spoken to will answer thee in the same way. Angry speech is painful: blows for blows will touch thee.

If, like a shattered metal plate (gong), thou utter nothing, then thou hast reached Nirvâna; anger is not known to thee.

As a cowherd with his staff drives his cows into the stable, so do Age and Death drive the life of men.

A fool does not know when he commits his evil deeds: but the wicked man burns by his own deeds, as if burned by fire.

He who inflicts pain on innocent and harmless persons, will soon come to one of these ten states—

He will have cruel suffering, loss, injury of the body, heavy affliction, or loss of mind.

A misfortune coming from the king, or a fearful accusation, or loss of relations, or destruction of treasures.

Lightning-fire will burn his houses; and when his body is destroyed, the fool will go to hell.

Not nakedness, not platted hair, not dirt, not fasting, or lying on the earth, not rubbing with dust, not sitting motionless, can purify a mortal who has not overcome desires.

He who, though dressed in fine apparel, exercises tranquility, is quiet, subdued, restrained, chaste, and has ceased to find fault with all other beings, he indeed is a Brâhmana, an ascetic (sramana), a friar (bhikshu).

Is there in this world any man so restrained by shame that he does not provoke reproof, as a noble horse the whip?

Like a noble horse when touched by the whip, be ye strenuous and eager, and by faith, by virtue, by energy, by meditation, by discernment of the law you will overcome this great pain, perfect in knowledge and in behavior, and never forgetful.

Well-makers lead the water wherever they like; fletchers bend the arrow; carpenters bend a log of wood; good people fashion themselves.

CHAPTER XI

OLD AGE

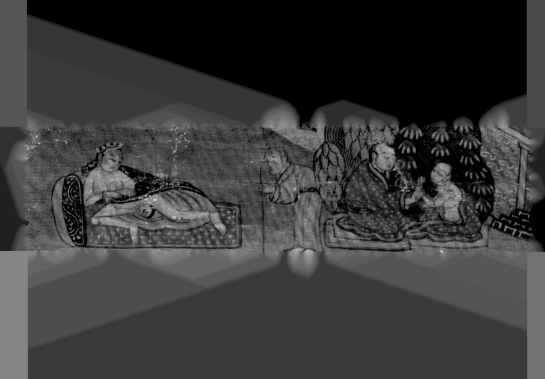

How is there laughter, how is there joy, as this world is always burning? Do you not seek a light, ye who are surrounded by darkness?

Look at this dressed-up lump, covered with wounds, joined together, sickly, full of many schemes, which has no strength, no hold!

This body is wasted, full of sickness, and frail; this heap of corruption breaks to pieces, life indeed ends in death.

After one has looked at those gray bones,
thrown away like gourds in the autumn,
what pleasure is there left in life!

After a stronghold has been made of
the bones, it is covered with flesh and
blood, and there dwell in it old age and
death, pride and deceit.

The brilliant chariots of kings are destroyed, the body also approaches destruction, but the virtue of good people never approaches destruction—thus do the good say to the good.

A man who has learned little, grows old like an ox; his flesh grows, but his knowledge does not grow.

Looking for the maker of this tabernacle, I shall have to run through a course of many births, not finding him; and painful is birth again and again. But now, maker of the tabernacle, thou hast been seen; thou shalt not make up this tabernacle again. All thy rafters are broken, thy ridgepole is sundered; the mind, approaching the Eternal (visankhâra, nirvâna), has attained to the extinction of all desires.

Men who have not observed proper discipline, and have not gained wealth in their youth, perish like old herons in a lake without fish.

Men who have not observed proper discipline, and have not gained wealth in their youth, lie, like broken bows, sighing after the past.

CHAPTER XII

SELF

If a man hold himself dear, let him watch himself carefully; during one at least out of the three watches a wise man should be watchful.

Let each man direct himself first to what is proper, then let him teach others; thus a wise man will not suffer.

If a man make himself as he teaches others to be, then, being himself well subdued, he may subdue others; for one's own self is indeed difficult to subdue.

Self is the lord of self, who else could be the lord? With self well subdued, a man finds a lord such as few can find.

The evil done by one's self, self-begotten, self-bred, crushes the foolish, as a diamond breaks even a precious stone.

He whose wickedness is very great brings himself down to that state where his enemy wishes him to be, as a creeper does with the tree which it surrounds.

Bad deeds, and deeds hurtful to ourselves, are easy to do; what is beneficial and good, that is very difficult to do.

The foolish man who scorns the rule of the venerable (Arhat), of the elect (Ariya), of the virtuous, and follows false doctrine, he bears fruit to his own destruction, like the fruits of the Katthaka reed.

By one's self the evil is done, by one's self one suffers; by one's self evil is left undone, by one's self one is purified. The pure and the impure stand and fall by themselves, no one can purify another.

Let no one forget his own duty for the sake of another's, however great; let a man, after he has discerned his own duty, be always attentive to his duty.

CHAPTER XIII

THE
WORLD

Do not follow the evil law! Do not live on in thoughtlessness! Do not follow false doctrine! Be not a friend of the world.

Rouse thyself! Do not be idle! Follow the law of virtue! The virtuous rests in bliss in this world and in the next.

Follow the law of virtue; do not follow that of sin. The virtuous rest in bliss in this world and in the next.

Look upon the world as you would on a bubble, look upon it as you would on a mirage: the king of death does not see him who thus looks down upon the world.

Come, look at this glittering world, like unto a royal chariot; the foolish are immersed in it, but the wise do not touch it.

He who formerly was reckless and afterwards became sober, brightens up this world, like the moon when freed from clouds.

He whose evil deeds are covered by good deeds, brightens up this world, like the moon when freed from clouds.

174

This world is dark, few only can see here; a few only go to heaven, like birds escaped from the net.

175

The swans go on the path of the sun, they go miraculously through the ether; the wise are led out of this world, when they have conquered Mâra and his train.

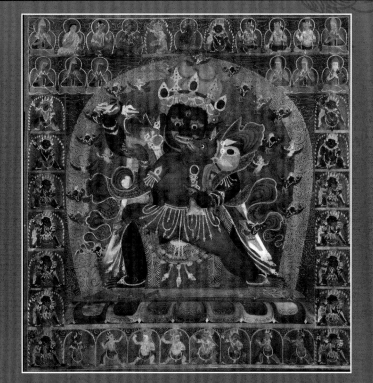

If a man has transgressed the one law, and speaks lies, and scoffs at another world, there is no evil he will not do.

The uncharitable do not go to the world of the gods; fools only do not praise liberality; a wise man rejoices in liberality, and through it becomes blessed in the other world.

Better than sovereignty over the earth, better than going to heaven, better than lordship over all worlds, is the reward of sotâpatti, the first step in holiness.

CHAPTER XIV

THE BUDDHA

(THE AWAKENED)

179

He whose conquest cannot be conquered again, into whose conquest no one in this world enters, by what track can you lead him, the Awakened, the Omniscient, the trackless?

180

He whom no desire with its snares and poisons can lead astray, by what track can you lead him, the Awakened, the Omniscient, the trackless?

Even the gods envy those who are awakened and not forgetful, who are given to meditation, who are wise, and who delight in the repose of retirement from the world.

Difficult to obtain is the conception of men, difficult is the life of mortals, difficult is the hearing of the True Law, difficult is the birth of the Awakened (the attainment of Buddhahood).

Not to commit any sin, to do good, and to purify one's mind, that is the teaching of all the Awakened.

The Awakened call patience the highest penance, long-suffering the highest Nirvâna; for he is not an anchorite (pravragita) who strikes others, he is not an ascetic (sramana) who insults others.

Not to blame, not to strike, to live restrained under the law, to be moderate in eating, to sleep and sit alone, and to dwell on the highest thoughts,—this is the teaching of the Awakened.

There is no satisfying lusts, even by a shower of gold pieces; he who knows that lusts have a short taste and cause pain, he is wise;

Even in heavenly pleasures he finds no satisfaction, the disciple who is fully awakened delights only in the destruction of all desires.

Men, driven by fear, go to many a refuge, to mountains and forests, to groves and sacred trees.

But that is not a safe refuge, that is not the best refuge; a man is not delivered from all pains after having gone to that refuge.

He who takes refuge with Buddha, the Law, and the Church; he who, with clear understanding, sees the four holy truths:

Pain, the origin of pain, the destruction of pain, and the eightfold holy way that leads to the quieting of pain.

That is the safe refuge, that is the best refuge; having gone to that refuge, a man is delivered from all pain.

A supernatural person (a Buddha) is not easily found, he is not born everywhere. Wherever such a sage is born, that race prospers.

Happy is the arising of the awakened, happy is the teaching of the True Law, happy is peace in the church, happy is the devotion of those who are at peace.

He who pays homage to those who deserve homage, whether the awakened (Buddha) or their disciples, those who have overcome the host of evils, and crossed the flood of sorrow, he who pays homage to such as have found deliverance and know no fear, his merit can never be measured by anyone.

CHAPTER XV

HAPPINESS

We live happily indeed, not hating those who hate us! among men who hate us let us dwell free from hatred!

We live happily indeed, free from ailments among the ailing! among men who are ailing let us dwell free from ailments!

We live happily indeed, free from greed among the greedy! among men who are greedy let us dwell free from greed!

We live happily indeed, though we call nothing our own! We shall be like the bright gods, feeding on happiness!

Victory breeds hatred, for the conquered is unhappy. He who has given up both victory and defeat, he, the contented, is happy.

There is no fire like passion; there is no losing throw like hatred; there is no pain like this body; there is no happiness higher than rest.

Hunger is the worst of diseases, the elements of the body the greatest evil; if one knows this truly, that is Nirvâna, the highest happiness.

Health is the greatest of gifts, contentedness the best riches; trust is the best of relationships, Nirvâna the highest happiness.

205

He who has tasted the sweetness of solitude and tranquillity, is free from fear and free from sin, while he tastes the sweetness of drinking in the law.

The sight of the elect (Arya) is good, to live with them is always happiness; if a man does not see fools, he will be truly happy.

He who walks in the company of fools suffers a long way; company with fools, as with an enemy, is always painful; company with the wise is pleasure, like meeting with kinsfolk.

Therefore, one ought to follow the wise, the intelligent, the learned, the much enduring, the dutiful, the elect; one ought to follow a good and wise man, as the moon follows the path of the stars.

CHAPTER XVI

PLEASURE

He who gives himself to vanity, and does not give himself to meditation, forgetting the real aim of life and grasping at pleasure, will in time envy him who has exerted himself in meditation.

Let no man cling to what is pleasant, or to what is unpleasant. Not to see what is pleasant is pain, and it is pain to see what is unpleasant.

Let, therefore, no man love anything; loss of the beloved is evil. Those who love nothing and hate nothing, have no fetters.

From pleasure comes grief, from pleasure comes fear; he who is free from pleasure knows neither grief nor fear.

From affection comes grief, from affection comes fear; he who is free from affection knows neither grief nor fear.

From lust comes grief, from lust comes fear; he who is free from lust knows neither grief nor fear.

From love comes grief, from love comes fear; he who is free from love knows neither grief nor fear.

From greed comes grief, from greed comes fear; he who is free from greed knows neither grief nor fear.

He who possesses virtue and intelligence, who is just, speaks the truth, and does what is his own business, him the world will hold dear.

He in whom a desire for the Ineffable (Nirvâna) has sprung up, who in his mind is satisfied, and whose thoughts are not bewildered by love, he is called ûrdhvamsrotas (carried upwards by the stream).

Kinsmen, friends, and lovers salute a man who has been long away, and returns safe from afar.

In like manner his good works receive him who has done good, and has gone from this world to the other;— as kinsmen receive a friend on his return.

CHAPTER XVII

ANGER

221

Let a man leave anger, let him forsake pride, let him overcome all bondage! No sufferings befall the man who is not attached to name and form, and who calls nothing his own.

222

He who holds back rising anger like a rolling chariot, him I call a real driver; other people are but holding the reins.

Let a man overcome anger by love, let him overcome evil by good; let him overcome the greedy by liberality, the liar by truth!

Speak the truth, do not yield to anger; give, if thou art asked for little; by these three steps thou wilt go near the gods.

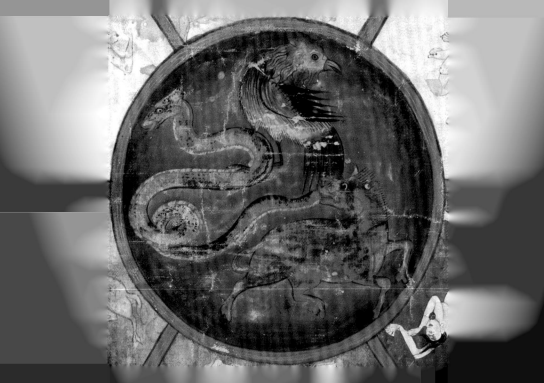

The sages who injure nobody, and who always control their body, they will go to the unchangeable place (Nirvâna), where, if they have gone, they will suffer no more.

Those who are ever watchful, who study day and night, and who strive after Nirvâna, their passions will come to an end.

This is an old saying, O Atula, this is not only of today: "They blame him who sits silent, they blame him who speaks much, they also blame him who says little; there is no one on earth who is not blamed."

There never was, there never will be, nor is there now, a man who is always blamed, or a man who is always praised.

But he whom those who discriminate praise continually day after day, as without blemish, wise, rich in knowledge and virtue, who would dare to blame him, like a coin made of gold from the Gambû river? Even the gods praise him, he is praised even by Brâhman.

Beware of bodily anger, and control thy body! Leave the sins of the body, and with thy body practice virtue!

Beware of the anger of the tongue, and control thy tongue! Leave the sins of the tongue, and practice virtue with thy tongue!

Beware of the anger of the mind, and control thy mind! Leave the sins of the mind, and practice virtue with thy mind!

The wise who control their body, who control their tongue, the wise who control their mind, are indeed well controlled.

CHAPTER XVIII

IMPURITY

Thou art now like a sear leaf, the messengers of death (Yama) have come near to thee; thou standest at the door of thy departure, and thou hast no provision for thy journey.

Make thyself an island, work hard, be wise! When thy impurities are blown away, and thou art free from guilt, thou wilt enter into the heavenly world of the elect (Ariya).

Thy life has come to an end, thou art come near to death (Yama), there is no resting-place for thee on the road, and thou hast no provision for thy journey.

Make thyself an island, work hard, be wise! When thy impurities are blown away, and thou art free from guilt, thou wilt not enter again into birth and decay.

Let a wise man blow off the impurities of himself, as a smith blows off the impurities of silver one by one, little by little, and from time to time.

As the impurity which springs from the iron, when it springs from it, destroys it; thus do a transgressor's own works lead him to the evil path.

241

The taint of prayers is non-repetition; the taint of houses, non-repair; the taint of complexion is sloth; the taint of a watchman, thoughtlessness.

242

Bad conduct is the taint of woman, greediness the taint of a benefactor; tainted are all evil ways in this world and in the next.

243

But there is a taint worse than all taints—ignorance is the greatest taint. O mendicants! throw off that taint, and become taintless!

244

Life is easy to live for a man who is without shame: a crow hero, a mischief-maker, an insulting, bold, and wretched fellow.

245

But life is hard to live for a modest man, who always looks for what is pure, who is disinterested, quiet, spotless, and intelligent.

He who destroys life, who speaks untruth, who in this world takes what is not given him, who goes to another man's wife;

And the man who gives himself to drinking intoxicating liquors, he, even in this world, digs up his own root.

O man, know this, that the unrestrained are in a bad state; take care that greediness and vice do not bring thee to grief for a long time!

The world gives according to their faith or according to their pleasure: if a man frets about the food and the drink given to others, he will find no rest either by day or by night.

He in whom that feeling is destroyed, and taken out with the very root, finds rest by day and by night.

251

There is no fire like passion, there is no shark like hatred, there is no snare like folly, there is no torrent like greed.

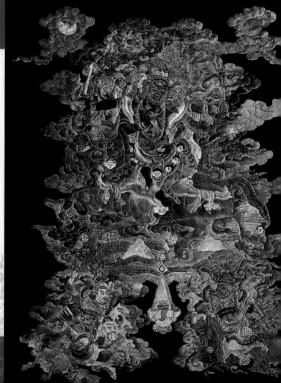

The fault of others is easily perceived, but that of one's self is difficult to perceive; a man winnows his neighbor's faults like chaff, but his own fault he hides, as a cheat hides the bad die from the player.

If a man looks after the faults of others, and is always inclined to be offended, his own passions will grow, and he is far from the destruction of passions.

There is no path through the air, a man is not a Samana outwardly. The world delights in vanity, the Tathâgatas (the Buddhas) are free from vanity.

There is no path through the air, a man is not a Samana outwardly. No creatures are eternal; but the awakened (Buddha) are never shaken.

CHAPTER XIX

THE
JUST

A man is not just if he carries a matter by violence; no, he who distinguishes both right and wrong, who is learned and leads others, not by violence, but by law and equity, and who is guarded by the law and intelligent, he is called just.

A man is not learned because he talks much; he who is patient, free from hatred and fear, he is called learned.

A man is not a supporter of the law because he talks much; even if a man has learned little, but sees the law bodily, he is a supporter of the law, a man who never neglects the law.

A man is not an elder because his head is gray; his age may be ripe, but he is called "Old-in-vain."

He in whom there is truth, virtue, love, restraint, moderation, he who is free from impurity and is wise, he is called an elder.

262

An envious, stingy, dishonest man does not become respectable by means of much talking only, or by the beauty of his complexion.

263

He in whom all this is destroyed, and taken out with the very root, he, when freed from hatred, is called respectable.

Not by tonsure does an undisciplined man who speaks falsehood become a Samana; can a man be a Samana who is still held captive by desire and greediness?

He who always quiets the evil, whether small or large, he is called a Samana (a quiet man), because he has quieted all evil.

266

A man is not a mendicant (Bhikshu) simply because he asks others for alms; he who adopts the whole law is a Bhikshu, not he who only begs.

267

He who is above good and evil, who is chaste, who with care passes through the world, he indeed is called a Bhikshu.

268

A man is not a Muni because he observes silence, if he is foolish and ignorant; but the wise who, as with the balance, chooses the good and avoids evil, he is a Muni, and is a Muni thereby; he who in this world weighs both sides is called a Muni.

270

A man is not an elect (Ariya) because he injures living creatures; because he has pity on all living creatures, therefore is a man called Ariya.

Not only by discipline and vows, not only by much learning, not by entering into a trance, not by sleeping alone, do I earn the happiness of release which no worldling can know. O Bhikshu, he who has obtained the extinction of desires, has obtained confidence.

CHAPTER XX

THE
WAY

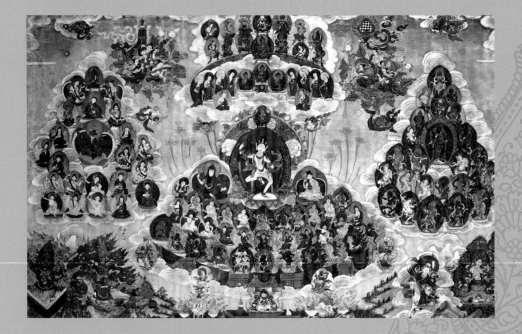

The best of ways is the eightfold; the best of truths the four words; the best of virtues passionlessness; the best of men he who has eyes to see.

This is the way, there is no other that leads to the purifying of intelligence. Go on this way! Everything else is the deceit of Mâra, the tempter.

If you go on this way, you will make an end of pain! The way was preached by me, when I had understood the removal of the thorns in the flesh.

You yourself must make an effort. The Tathâgatas (Buddhas) are only preachers. The thoughtful who enter the way are freed from the bondage of Mâra.

"All created things perish," he who knows and sees this becomes passive in pain; this is the way to purity.

"All created things are grief and pain," he who knows and sees this becomes passive in pain; this is the way that leads to purity.

"All forms are unreal," he who knows and sees this becomes passive in pain; this is the way that leads to purity.

280

He who does not rouse himself when it is time to rise, who, though young and strong, is full of sloth, whose will and thought are weak, that lazy and idle man will never find the way to knowledge.

281

Watching his speech, well restrained in mind, let a man never commit any wrong with his body! Let a man but keep these three roads of action clear, and he will achieve the way which is taught by the wise.

Through zeal knowledge is gained, through lack of zeal knowledge is lost; let a man who knows this double path of gain and loss thus place himself that knowledge may grow.

Cut down the whole forest of desires, not a tree only! Danger comes out of the forest of desires. When you have cut down both the forest of desires and its undergrowth, then, Bhikshus, you will be rid of the forest and of desires!

So long as the love of man towards women, even the smallest, is not destroyed, so long is his mind in bondage, as the calf that drinks milk is to its mother.

Cut out the love of self, like an autumn lotus, with thy hand! Cherish the road of peace. Nirvâna has been shown by Sugata (Buddha).

"Here I shall dwell in the rain, here in winter and summer," thus the fool meditates, and does not think of his death.

Death comes and carries off that man, praised for his children and flocks, his mind distracted, as a flood carries off a sleeping village.

Sons are no help, nor a father, nor relations; there is no help from kinsfolk for one whom death has seized.

A wise and good man who knows the meaning of this, should quickly clear the way that leads to Nirvâna.

MISCELLANEOUS

If by leaving a small pleasure one sees a great pleasure, let a wise man leave the small pleasure, and look to the great.

He who, by causing pain to others, wishes to obtain pleasure for himself, he, entangled in the bonds of hatred, will never be free from hatred.

292

What ought to be done is neglected, what ought not to be done is done; the desires of unruly, thoughtless people are always increasing.

293

But they whose whole watchfulness is always directed to their body, who do not follow what ought not to be done, and who steadfastly do what ought to be done, the desires of such watchful and wise people will come to an end.

A true Brâhmana goes scatheless, though he have killed father and mother, and two valiant kings, though he has destroyed a kingdom with all its subjects.

A true Brâhmana goes scatheless, though he have killed father and mother, and two holy kings, and an eminent man besides.

The disciples of Gotama (Buddha) are always well awake, and their thoughts day and night are always set on Buddha.

The disciples of Gotama are always well awake, and their thoughts day and night are always set on the law.

The disciples of Gotama are always well awake, and their thoughts day and night are always set on the church.

The disciples of Gotama are always well awake, and their thoughts day and night are always set on their body.

The disciples of Gotama are always well awake, and their mind day and night always delights in compassion.

The disciples of Gotama are always well awake, and their mind day and night always delights in meditation.

It is hard to leave the world to become a friar, it is hard to enjoy the world; hard is the monastery, painful are the houses; painful it is to dwell with equals to share everything in common and the itinerant mendicant is beset with pain. Therefore let no man be an itinerant mendicant and he will not be beset with pain.

A man full of faith, if endowed with virtue and glory, is respected, whatever place he may choose.

Good people shine from afar, like the snowy mountains; bad people are not seen, like arrows shot by night.

Sitting alone, lying down alone, walking without ceasing, and alone subduing himself, let a man be happy near the edge of a forest.

305

CHAPTER XXII

THE
DOWNWARD COURSE

He who says what is not, goes to hell; he also who, having done a thing, says I have not done it. After death both are equal, they are men with evil deeds in the next world.

Many men whose shoulders are covered with the yellow gown are ill-conditioned and unrestrained; such evildoers by their evil deeds go to hell.

Better it would be to swallow a heated iron ball, like flaring fire, than that a bad unrestrained fellow should live on the charity of the land.

Four things does a wreckless man gain who covets his neighbor's wife—demerit, an uncomfortable bed, thirdly, punishment, and lastly, hell.

There is demerit, and the evil way to hell, there is the short pleasure of the frightened in the arms of the frightened, and the king imposes heavy punishment; therefore let no man think of his neighbor's wife.

As a grass-blade, if badly grasped, cuts the arm, badly practiced asceticism leads to hell.

An act carelessly performed, a broken vow, and hesitating obedience to discipline (Brâhma-kariyam), all this brings no great reward.

If anything is to be done, let a man do, let him attack it vigorously! A careless pilgrim only scatters the dust of his passions more widely.

An evil deed is better left undone, for a man repents of it afterwards; a good deed is better done, for having done it, one does not repent.

Like a well-guarded frontier fort, with defenses within and without, so let a man guard himself. Not a moment should escape, for they who allow the right moment to pass, suffer pain when they are in hell.

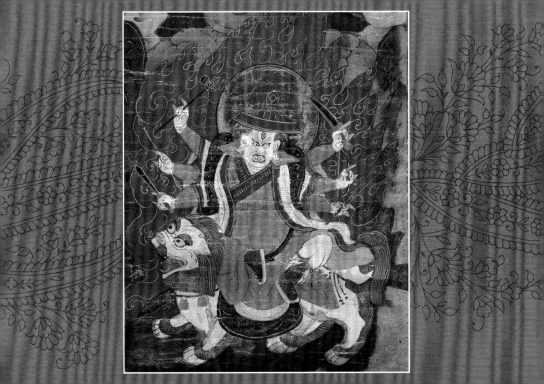

They who are ashamed of what they ought not to be ashamed of, and are not ashamed of what they ought to be ashamed of, such men, embracing false doctrines, enter the evil path.

They who fear when they ought not to fear, and fear not when they ought to fear, such men, embracing false doctrines, enter the evil path.

They who see sin where there is no sin, and see no sin where there is sin, such men, embracing false doctrines, enter the evil path.

They who see sin where there is no sin, and see no sin where there is sin, such men, embracing the true doctrine, enter the good path.

CHAPTER XXIII

THE
ELEPHANT

Silently I endured abuse as the elephant in battle endures the arrow sent from the bow: for the world is ill-natured.

They lead a tamed elephant to battle, the king mounts a tamed elephant; the tamed is the best among men, he who silently endures abuse.

Mules are good, if tamed, and noble Sindhu horses, and elephants with large tusks; but he who tames himself is better still.

For with these animals does no man reach the untrodden country (Nirvâna), where a tamed man goes on a tamed animal—on his own well-tamed self.

The elephant called Dhanapâlaka, his temples running with pungent sap, and who is difficult to hold, does not eat a morsel when bound; the elephant longs for the elephant grove.

If a man becomes fat and a great eater, if he is sleepy and rolls himself about, that fool, like a hog fed on grains, is born again and again.

This mind of mine went formerly wandering about as it liked, as it listed, as it pleased; but I shall now hold it in thoroughly, as the rider who holds the hook holds in the furious elephant.

Be not thoughtless, watch your thoughts! Draw yourself out of the evil way, like an elephant sunk in mud.

If a man find a prudent companion who walks with him, is wise, and lives soberly, he may walk with him, overcoming all dangers, happy, but considerate.

If a man find no prudent companion who walks with him, is wise, and lives soberly, let him walk alone, like a king who has left his conquered country behind—like an elephant in the forest.

It is better to live alone: there is no companionship with a fool; let a man walk alone, let him commit no sin, with few wishes, like an elephant in the forest.

331

If an occasion arises, friends are pleasant; enjoyment is pleasant, whatever be the cause; a good work is pleasant in the hour of death; the giving up of all grief is pleasant.

332

Pleasant in the world is the state of a mother, pleasant the state of a father, pleasant the state of a Samana, pleasant the state of a Brâhmana.

333

Pleasant is virtue lasting to old age, pleasant is a faith firmly rooted; pleasant is attainment of intelligence, pleasant is avoiding of sins.

CHAPTER XXIV

THIRST

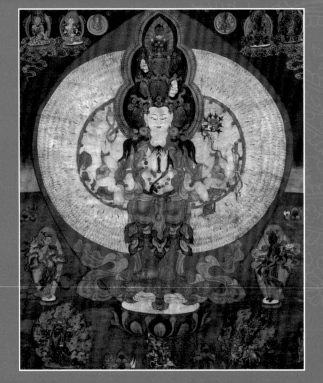

The thirst of a thoughtless man grows like a creeper; he runs from life to life, like a monkey seeking fruit in the forest.

Whomsoever this fierce thirst overcomes, full of poison, in this world, his sufferings increase like the abounding Bírana grass.

But from him who overcomes this fierce thirst, difficult to be conquered in this world, sufferings fall off, like water-drops from a lotus leaf.

This salutary word I tell you, "Do ye, as many as are here assembled, dig up the root of thirst, as he who wants the sweet-scented Usíra root must dig up the Birana grass, that Mâra, the tempter, may not crush you again and again, as the stream crushes the reeds."

As a tree, even though it has been cut down, is firm so long as its root is safe, and grows again, thus, unless the feeders of thirst are destroyed, the pain of life will return again and again.

He whose thirty-six streams are strongly flowing in the channels of pleasure, the waves—his desires which are set on passion—will carry away that misguided man.

The channels run everywhere, the creeper of passion stands sprouting; if you see the creeper springing up, cut its root by means of knowledge.

A creature's pleasures are extravagant and luxurious; given up to pleasure and deriving happiness, men undergo again and again birth and decay.

Beset with lust, men run about like a snared hare; held in fetters and bonds, they undergo pain for a long time, again and again.

Beset with lust, men run about like a snared hare; let therefore the mendicant drive out thirst, by striving after passionlessness for himself.

He who having got rid of the forest of lust (after having reached Nirvâna) gives himself over to forest-life (to lust), and who, when removed from the forest (from lust), runs to the forest (to lust), look at that man! Though free, he runs into bondage.

Wise people do not call that a strong fetter which is made of iron, wood, or hemp; far stronger is the care for precious stones and rings, for sons and a wife.

That fetter wise people call strong which drags down, yields, but is difficult to undo; after having cut this at last, people leave the world, free from cares, and leaving desires and pleasures of love behind.

Those who are slaves to passions, run down with the stream of desires, as a spider runs down the web which he has made himself; when they have cut this, at last, wise people go onwards, free from cares, leaving all pain behind.

Give up what is before, give up what is behind, give up what is between, when thou goest to the other shore of existence; if thy mind is altogether free, thou wilt not again enter into birth and decay.

If a man is tossed about by doubts, full of strong passions, and yearning only for what is delightful, his thirst will grow more and more, and he will indeed make his fetters strong.

If a man delights in quieting doubts, and, always reflecting, dwells on what is not delightful, he certainly will remove, nay, he will cut the fetter of Mâra.

He who has reached the consummation, who does not tremble, who is without thirst and without sin, he has broken all the thorns of life: this will be his last body.

He who is without thirst and without affection, who understands the words and their interpretation, who knows the order of letters (those which are before and which are after), he has received his last body, he is called the great sage, the great man.

"I have conquered all, I know all, in all conditions of life I am free from taint; I have left all, and through the destruction of thirst I am free; having learned myself, whom should I indicate as my teacher?"

The gift of the law exceeds all gifts; the sweetness of the law exceeds all sweetness; the delight in the law exceeds all delights; the extinction of thirst overcomes all pain.

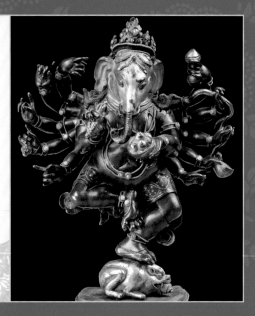

355

Riches destroy the foolish, if they look not for the other shore; the foolish by his thirst for riches destroys himself, as if he were destroying others.

The fields are damaged by weeds, mankind is damaged by passion: therefore a gift bestowed on the passionless brings great reward.

The fields are damaged by weeds, mankind is damaged by hatred: therefore a gift bestowed on those who do not hate brings great reward.

The fields are damaged by weeds, mankind is damaged by vanity: therefore a gift bestowed on those who are free from vanity brings great reward.

The fields are damaged by weeds, mankind is damaged by lust: therefore a gift bestowed on those who are free from lust brings great reward.

CHAPTER XXV

THE
BHIKSHU
(MENDICANT)

Restraint in the eye is good, good is restraint in the ear, in the nose restraint is good, good is restraint in the tongue.

In the body restraint is good, good is restraint in speech, in thought restraint is good, good is restraint in all things. A Bhikshu, restrained in all things, is freed from all pain.

He who controls his hand, he who controls his feet, he who controls his speech, he who is well controlled, he who delights inwardly, who is collected, who is solitary and content, him they call Bhikshu.

The Bhikshu who controls his mouth, who speaks wisely and calmly, who teaches the meaning and the law, his word is sweet.

He who dwells in the law, delights in the law, meditates on the law, follows the law, that Bhikshu will never fall away from the true law.

Let him not despise what he has received, nor ever envy others: a mendicant who envies others does not obtain peace of mind.

A Bhikshu who, though he receives little, does not despise what he has received, even the gods will praise him, if his life is pure, and if he is not slothful.

He who never identifies himself with name and form, and does not grieve over what is no more, he indeed is called a Bhikshu.

The Bhikshu who behaves with kindness, who is happy in the doctrine of Buddha, will reach the quiet place (Nirvâna), happiness arising from the cessation of natural inclinations.

O Bhikshu, empty this boat! If emptied, it will go quickly; having cut off passion and hatred, thou wilt go to Nirvâna.

Cut off the five fetters, leave the five, rise above the five. A Bhikshu, who has escaped from the five fetters, he is called Oghatinna—"saved from the flood."

Meditate, O Bhikshu, and be not heedless! Do not direct thy thought to what gives pleasure that thou mayest not for thy heedlessness have to swallow the iron ball in hell, and that thou mayest not cry out when burning, "This is pain."

Without knowledge there is no meditation, without meditation there is no knowledge: he who has knowledge and meditation is near unto Nirvâna.

A Bhikshu who has entered his empty house, and whose mind is tranquil, feels a more than human delight when he sees the law clearly.

As soon as he has considered the origin and destruction of the elements of the body, he finds happiness and joy which belong to those who know the immortal (Nirvâna).

And this is the beginning here for a wise Bhikshu: watchfulness over the senses, contentedness, restraint under the law; keep noble friends whose life is pure, and who are not slothful.

Let him live in charity, let him be perfect in his duties; then in the fullness of delight he will make an end of suffering.

As the Vassikâ plant sheds its withered flowers, men should shed passion and hatred, O ye Bhikshus!

The Bhikshu whose body and tongue and mind are quieted, who is collected, and has rejected the baits of the world, he is called quiet.

Rouse thyself by thyself, examine thyself by thyself, thus self-protected and attentive wilt thou live happily, O Bhikshu!

For self is the lord of self, self is the refuge of self; therefore curb thyself as the merchant curbs a noble horse.

The Bhikshu, full of delight, who is happy in the doctrine of Buddha will reach the quiet place (Nirvâna), happiness consisting in the cessation of natural inclinations.

He who, even as a young Bhikshu, applies himself to the doctrine of Buddha, brightens up this world, like the moon when free from clouds.

THE
BRÂHMANA
(ARHAT)

Stop the stream valiantly, drive away the desires, O Brâhmana! When you have understood the destruction of all that was made, you will understand that which was not made.

If the Brâhmana has reached the other shore in both laws, in restraint and contemplation, all bonds vanish from him who has obtained knowledge.

He for whom there is neither the hither nor the further shore, nor both, him, the fearless and unshackled, I call indeed a Brâhmana.

He who is thoughtful, blameless, settled, dutiful, without passions, and who has attained the highest end, him I call indeed a Brâhmana.

The sun is bright by day, the moon shines by night, the warrior is bright in his armor, the Brâhmana is bright in his meditation; but Buddha, the Awakened, is bright with splendor day and night.

Because a man is rid of evil, therefore he is called Brâhmana; because he walks quietly, therefore he is called Samana; because he has sent away his own impurities, therefore he is called Pravragita (Pabbagita, a pilgrim).

No one should attack a Brâhmana, but no Brâhmana if attacked, should let himself fly at his aggressor! Woe to him who strikes a Brâhmana, more woe to him who flies at his aggressor!

It advantages a Brâhmana not a little if he holds his mind back from the pleasures of life; when all wish to injure has vanished, the more pain will cease.

Him I call indeed a Brâhmana who does not offend by body, word, or thought, and is controlled on these three points.

He from whom he may learn the law, as taught by the Well-awakened (Buddha), let him worship it assiduously, as the Brâhmana worships the sacrificial fire.

A man does not become a Brâhmana by his platted hair, by his family, or by birth; in whom there is truth and righteousness, he is blessed, he is a Brâhmana.

What is the use of platted hair, O fool! what of the raiment of goat-skins? Within thee there is ravening, but the outside thou makest clean.

The man who wears dirty raiments, who is emaciated and covered with veins, who lives alone in the forest, and meditates, him I call indeed a Brâhmana.

I do not call a man a Brâhmana because of his origin or of his mother. He is indeed arrogant, and he is wealthy: but the poor, who is free from all attachments, him I call indeed a Brâhmana.

Him I call indeed a Brâhmana who, after cutting all fetters, never trembles, is free from bonds and unshackled.

Him I call indeed a Brâhmana who, after cutting the strap and the thong, the rope with all that pertains to it, has destroyed all obstacles, and is awakened.

Him I call indeed a Brahmana who, though he has committed no offense, endures reproach, stripes, and bonds: who has endurance for his force, and strength for his army.

Him I call indeed a Brâhmana who is free from anger, dutiful, virtuous, without appetite, who is subdued, and has received his last body.

Him I call indeed a Brâhmana who does not cling to sensual pleasures, like water on a lotus leaf, like a mustard seed on the point of a needle.

Him I call indeed a Brâhmana who, even here, knows the end of his own suffering, has put down his burden, and is unshackled.

Him I call indeed a Brâhmana whose knowledge is deep, who possesses wisdom, who knows the right way and the wrong, and has attained the highest end.

Him I call indeed a Brâhmana who keeps aloof both from laymen and from mendicants, who frequents no houses, and has but few desires.

Him I call indeed a Brâhmana who without hurting any creatures, whether feeble or strong, does not kill nor cause slaughter.

Him I call indeed a Brâhmana who is tolerant with the intolerant, mild with the violent, and free from greed among the greedy.

Him I call indeed a Brâhmana from whom anger and hatred, pride and envy have dropped like a mustard seed from the point of a needle.

Him I call indeed a Brâhmana who utters true speech, instructive and free from harshness, so that he offend no one.

Him I call indeed a Brâhmana who takes nothing in the world that is not given him, be it long or short, small or large, good or bad.

Him I call indeed a Brâhmana who fosters no desires for this world or for the next, has no inclinations, and is unshackled.

Him I call indeed a Brâhmana who has no interests, and when he has understood the truth, does not say How, how? and who has reached the depth of the Immortal.

Him I call indeed a Brâhmana who in this world has risen above both ties, good and evil, who is free from grief, from sin, and from impurity.

Him I call indeed a Brâhmana who is bright like the moon, pure, serene, undisturbed, and in whom all gaiety is extinct.

Him I call indeed a Brâhmana who has traversed this miry road, the impassable world, difficult to pass, and its vanity, who has gone through, and reached the other shore, is thoughtful, steadfast, free from doubts, free from attachment, and content.

Him I call indeed a Brâhmana who in this world, having abandoned all desires, travels about without a home, and in whom all concupiscence is extinct.

Him I call indeed a Brâhmana who, leaving all longings, travels about without a home, and in whom all covetousness is extinct.

Him I call indeed a Brâhmana who, after leaving all bondage to men, has risen above all bondage to the gods, and is free from all and every bondage.

Him I call indeed a Brâhmana who has left what gives pleasure and what gives pain, who is cold, and free from all germs: of renewed life, the hero who has conquered all the worlds.

Him I call indeed a Brâhmana who knows the destruction and the return of beings everywhere, who is free from bondage, welfaring (Sugata), and awakened (Buddha).

Him I call indeed a Brâhmana whose path the gods do not know, nor spirits (Gandharvas), nor men, whose passions are extinct, and who is an Arhat.

Him I call indeed a Brâhmana who calls nothing his own, whether it be before, behind, or between; who is poor, and free from the love of the world.

Him I call indeed a Brâhmana, the manly, the noble, the hero, the great sage, the conqueror, the indifferent, the accomplished, the awakened.

423

Him I call indeed a Brâhmana who knows his former abodes, who sees heaven and hell, has reached the end of births, is perfect in knowledge, a sage, and whose perfections are all perfect.

LIST OF ILLUSTRATIONS

Page 8
Eight Mahasiddha, detail
Eastern Tibet, 18th century
ground mineral pigment on cotton

Page 11
Virudhaka, Guardian of the South
Tibet, 18th century
ground mineral pigment on cotton

Page 12
Karma Lingpa Shitro manuscript
Mongolia, 19th century
ground miner pigment on paper

Page 13
Dorje Shugden
Tibet, 19th century
ground mineral pigment, fine gold line
on cotton

Page 14
Vajrayogini
Tibet, 18th century
ground mineral pigment on cotton

Page 15
Drog Dze Wangmo
Tibet, 19th century
ground mineral pigment, fine gold line
on cotton

Page 16
Avadana (Teaching Stories) #12, detail
Eastern Tibet, 19th century
ground mineral pigment on cotton

Page 17
Wheel of Life, detail
Eastern Tibet, 18th century
ground mineral pigment, fine gold line
cotton

Page 19
Bodhisattva Kunto Zangpo
Tibet, 18th century
ground mineral pigment on cotton

Page 22
Buddha Amitayus
Mongolia, 17th century
metal

Page 25
Arhat Bhadra
Eastern Tibet, 19th century
ground mineral pigment on cotton

Page 25
Stupa, detail
Nepal, 18th century
ground mineral pigment on cotton

Page 27
Chaturbhuja Avalokiteshvara Mandala
Tibet, 18th century
ground mineral pigment on cotton

Page 28
Buddha Shakyamuni
Tibet, 19th century
ground mineral pigment on cotton

Page 31
Shri Hevajra and the Eight Goddesses
Tibet, 18th century
ground mineral pigment on cotton

Page 33
Buddha Vajradhara
Tibet, 15th century
ground mineral pigment, raised gold
on cotton

Page 34
Virudhaka, Guardian of the South
Tibet, 14th century
ground mineral pigment on cotton

Page 35
Shadbhuja Vajra Mahakala, detail
Tibet, 19th century
ground mineral pigment, fine gold
line, black background on cotton

Page 36
Pehar, King of Qualities
Central Tibet, 19th century
ground mineral pigment, fine gold line
on cotton

Page 40
Wheel of Life
Mongolia, 19th century
ground mineral pigment, fine gold line
on cotton

Page 42
Mahasiddha Ghantapa
Eastern Tibet, 19th century
ground mineral pigment, fine gold line
on cotton

Page 43
King of Shambhala
Eastern Tibet, 19th century
ground mineral pigment, fine gold line
on cotton

Page 45
Buddha Amitabha
Central Tibet, 19th century
ground mineral pigment on cotton

Page 46
Shadbhuja Mahakala
Eastern Tibet, 19th century
ground mineral pigment on cotton

Page 50
Arhat Dharmata
Tibet, 19th century
ground mineral pigment on cotton

Page 51
Red Jambhala
Tibet
ground mineral pigment on cotton

Page 52
Mahasiddha Damarupa, detail
Eastern Tibet, 18th century
ground mineral pigment on cotton

Page 55
Lama Tsongkhapa, detail
Tibet, 18th century
ground mineral pigment on cotton

Page 56
Parnashavari
Central Tibet, 18th century
ground mineral pigment, fine gold line
on cotton

Page 59
Shadbhuja Mahakala
Tibet, 18th century
ground mineral pigment on cotton

Page 62
Avadana (Teaching Stories) #12, detail
Eastern Tibet, 19th century
ground mineral pigment on cotton

Page 63
Kelzang Gyatso, 7th Dalai Lama
Tibet, 18th century
ground mineral pigment, fine gold line
on cotton

Page 64
Buddha Shakyamuni, detail
Eastern Tibet, 18th century
ground mineral pigment, fine gold line
on cotton

Page 65
Astrological Chart, detail
Tibet, 19th century
ground mineral pigment on cotton

Page 66
Avadana (Teaching Stories) #12, detail
Eastern Tibet, 19th century
ground mineral pigment on cotton

Page 67
Yama Dharmaraja
Tibet, 19th century
ground mineral pigment, fine gold line
on cotton

Page 68
Lama Pema Chogyal
Tibet, 19th century
ground mineral pigment, fine gold line
on cotton

Page 72
Arhat Dharmata
Eastern Tibet, 17th century
ground mineral pigment on cotton

Page 73
Arhat Bakula
Eastern Tibet, 19th century
ground mineral pigment on cotton

Page 74
Garuda
Tibet, 18th century
ground mineral pigment on cotton

Page 77
Arhat Ajita
Eastern Tibet, 18th century
ground mineral pigment on cotton

Page 80
Tsangyang Gyatso, 6th Dalai Lama
ground mineral pigment, red
background on cotton

Page 83
Dhritarashtra, Guardian of the East
Tibet, 17th century
ground mineral pigment on cotton

Page 84
Lama Gampopa
Tibet, 15th century
ground mineral pigment, fine gold line
on cotton

Page 86
White Tara
Eastern Tibet, 19th century
ground mineral pigment on cotton

Page 90
Simhamukha
18th century

Page 92
Srog Lha
Tibet, 19th century
ground mineral pigment on cottong

Page 93
Siddha Lakshmi
Himalayan region, 17th century
metal

Page 94
Ekajati, detail
Bhutan, 19th century
ground mineral pigment on cotton

Page 95
Shambhala Mandala
Tibet, 19th century
ground mineral pigment, fine gold line
on cotton

Page 98
Ashtabhya Tara
Eastern Tibet, 18th century
ground mineral pigment on cotton

Page 99
Bodhisattva Avalokiteshvara
Central Tibet, 17th century
fine gold line, red background on
cotton

Page 100
Wheel of Life, detail
Mongolia, 19th century
ground mineral pigment, fine gold line
on cotton

Page 101
Wheel of Life, detail
Eastern Tibet, 18th century
ground mineral pigment, fine gold line
on cotton

Page 103
Avadana (Teaching Stories) #19, detail
Eastern Tibet, 19th century
ground mineral pigment on cotton

Page 104
Mahasiddha Kanha of the East
Tibet, 16th century
metal

Page 106
Lama Gampopa
Tibet, 16th century
ground mineral pigment, fine gold line
on cotton

Page 107
Buddha Nagaraja
Tibet, 19th century
ground mineral pigment, fine gold line
on cotton

Page 110
Buddha Shakyamuni, detail
Tibet, 19th century
ground mineral pigment on cotton

Page 112
Ashtabhya Tara, detail
Eastern Tibet, 17th century
ground mineral pigment on cotton

Page 113
Avadana (Teaching Stories)
Eastern Tibet, 19th century
ground mineral pigment on cotton

Page 114
Vajrapani Mandala
Tibet, 15th century
ground mineral pigment on cotton

Page 115
Padmasambhava
Bhutan, 18th century
ground mineral pigment, fine gold line
on cotton

Page 117
Lama Dampa Sonam Gyaltsen
Tibet, 17th century
metal

Page 118
Vajrabhairava, detail
Central Tibet, 18th century
ground mineral pigment on silk

Page 120
Jataka (Previous Lives of Buddha
Shakyamuni)
Tibet, 18th century
ground mineral pigment on cotton

Page 123
Vajrapani Bhutadamara, detail
Tibet, 18th century
ground mineral pigment, fine gold line
on cotton

Page 126
Lama Tsongkhapa
Himalayan region, 19th century

metal

Page 128
Dorje Tragtsen, detail
Tibet, 18th century
ground mineral pigment, fine gold
line, black bacground on cotton

Page 129
Wangdu Nyingpo, Khon Tuchen
ground mineral pigment, fine gold line
on cotton

Page 131
Vajrapani and Consort
Tibet, 14th century
ground mineral pigment, fine gold line
on cotton

Page 132
Mahasiddha Virupa
Tibet, 17th century
ground mineral pigment on cotton

Page 136
Avadana (Teaching Stories) #16
Tibet
ground mineral pigment on cotton

Page 140
Buddha Akshobhya

Tibet, 13th century
bronze

Page 141
Avadana (Teaching Stories) #11
Tibet, 19th century
ground mineral pigment on cotton

Page 142
Simhanada Avalokiteshvara
Tibet, 19th century
ground mineral pigment on cotton

Page 145
Buddha Shakyamuni
India, 11th century
Bronze, copper inlay, silver inlay

Page 148
Simhamukha
Tibet, 18th century
embroidery, appliqué on textile

Page 151
Pancha Raksha
Tibet, 14th century
metal, turquoise inset

Page 153
Marichi

Mongolia, 17th century
metal, painted face and hair

Page 154
Red Jambhala, detail
Eastern Tibet, 19th century
ground mineral pigment on cotton

Page 158
Kakyab Dorje, 15th Karmapa
Eastern Tibet, 19th century
ground mineral pigment on cotton

Page 159
Lama Yutog Yontan Gonpo, detail
Tibet, 18th century
raised gold, red background on cotton

Page 160
Mahasiddha Virupa
Tibet, 15th century
ground mineral pigment on cotton

Page 162
Avadana (Teaching Stories) #19
Eastern Tibet, 19th century
ground mineral pigment on cotton

Page 163

Buddha Shakyamuni, detail
Tibet, 19th century
ground mineral pigment on cotton

Page 166
Green Tara Protecting from Fear of
Lions
Tibet, 19th century
ground mineral pigment on cotton

Page 167
Green Tara Protecting from Fear of
Fire
Tibet, 19th century
ground mineral pigment on cotton

Page 168
Wheel of Life, detail
Eastern Tibet, 18th century
ground mineral pigment, fine gold line
on cotton

Page 171
Buddha Amitayus
Central Tibet, 15th century
ground mineral pigment, fine gold
line, gold background on cotton

Page 172
Arya Asanga
Tibet, 19th century

ground mineral pigment on cotton

Page 176
Yama Dharmaraja
Central Tibet, 19th century
ground mineral pigment on cotton

Page 177
Green Tara Protecting from Fear of
Drowning
Tibet, 19th century
ground mineral pigment on cotton

Page 178
Green Tara Protecting from Fear of
Demons
Tibet, 19th century
ground mineral pigment on cotton

Page 181
Wheel of Life, detail
Eastern Tibet, 18th century
ground mineral pigment, fine gold line
on cotton

Page 182
Green Tara Protecting from Fear of
Thieves
Tibet, 19th century
ground mineral pigment on cotton

Page 185
Green Tara Protecting from Fear of
Wrongful Imprisonment
Tibet, 19th century
ground mineral pigment on cotton

Page 186
White Tara, detail
Eastern Tibet, 19th century
ground mineral pigment on cotton

Page 187
Sipai Gyalmo
China, 19th century
embroidery on textile

Page 188
Chaturbhuja Avalokiteshvara Mandala
Tibet, 18th century
ground mineral pigment on cotton

Page 189
Bodhisattvas Avalokiteshvara and
Maitreya
Tibet, 16th century
ground mineral pigment on cotton

Page 1928
Vajrakila Heruka
Tibet, 19th century
ground mineral pigment, black

background on cotton

Page 194
Arhats Ajita and Kanakavata
Tibet, 17th century
ground mineral pigment on cotton

Page 195
Buddha Shakyamuni
Tibet, 19th century
ground mineral pigment, fine gold line
on cotton

Page 196
Avadana (Teaching Stories) #12, detail
Eastern Tibet, 19th century
ground mineral pigment on cotton

Page 197
Guru Nyima Ozer
Eastern Tibet, 19th century
ground mineral pigment on cotton

Page 198
Machig Labdron, detail
Eastern Tibet, 19th century
ground mineral pigment on cotton

Page 199
Orange Tara Purifying All Poverty

Central Tibet, 18th century
ground mineral pigment on cotton

Page 202
Cho Lineage Refuge Field, detail
Tibet, 19th century
ground mineral pigment on cotton

Page 205
Rangjung Dorje, 3rd Karmapa
Eastern Tibet, 19th century
ground mineral pigment, fine gold line
on cotton

Page 206
Wangdu Nyingpo, Khon Tuchen
Tibet, 18th century
ground mineral pigment on cotton

Page 207
Sonam Tsemo and Jetsun Dragpa
Gyaltsen
Tibet, 16th century
ground mineral pigment, fine gold line
on cotton

Page 208
Dudul Dorje, 13th Karmapa
Eastern Tibet, 18th century
ground mineral pigment, fine gold line

on cotton

Page 209
Maitreya
Tibet, 17th century
fine gold line, red background on cotton

Page 210
Rakta Yamari Mandala
Tibet, 17th century
ground mineral pigment on cotton

Page 214
Arhats Bakula and Rahula
Central Tibet, 17th century
ground mineral pigment, fine gold line
on cotton

Page 215
Wangdu Nyingpo, Khon Tuchen
Tibet, early 20th century
ground mineral pigment on cotton

Page 216
Wangdu Nyinpo, Khon Tuchen
Tibet, 18th century
ground mineral pigment on cotton

Page 219
Chaturbhuja Avalokiteshvara
Tibet, 18th century
ground mineral pigment, raised gold,

fine gold line on cotton

Page 220
Buddha Shakyamuni
Eastern Tibet, 18th century
ground mineral pigment, fine gold line on cotton

Page 222
Tongwa Donden, 6th Karmapa
Eastern Tibet, early 20th century
ground mineral pigment on cotton

Page 223
Buddha Shakyamuni
Eastern Tibet, 16th century
ground mineral pigment on cotton

Page 225
Lama Tsongkhapa
Tibet, 18th century
ground mineral pigment on cotton

Page 229
Gyalpo Pehar
Tibet, 18th century
ground mineral pigment on cotton

Page 230
Ensapa Lobsang Döndrup, 3rd
Panchen Lama

China, 19th century
ground mineral pigment on cotton

Page 233
Gyalpo Pehar
Tibet, 18th century
ground mineral pigment on cotton

Page 234
Mahasiddha Avadhutipa
Eastern Tibet, 18th century
ground mineral pigment, fine gold line on cotton

Page 238
Jetsun Dragpa Gyaltsen
Central Tibet, 18th century
ground mineral pigment on cotton

Page 241
Gyalpo Pehar
Tibet, 19th century
ground mineral pigment on cotton

Page 242
Wrathful Offerings, detail
Mongolia, 19th century
ground mineral pigment on cotton

Page 245

Buddha Shakyamuni
Tibet, 18th century
ground mineral pigment on cotton

Page 246
Avadana (Teaching Stories) #12
Eastern Tibet, 19th century
ground mineral pigment on cotton

Page 250
Ekadashamukha Sahasrabhuja
Avalokiteshvara
Tibet, 18th century
ground mineral pigment, fine gold line on cotton

Page 253
King of Shambhala
Eastern Tibet, 18th century
ground mineral pigment, fine gold line on cotton

Page 254
Aryadeva
Tibet, 19th century
ground mineral pigment on cotton

Page 255
Buddha Shakyamuni
Tibet, 17th century

ground mineral pigment, fine gold line
on cotton

Page 256
Chaturbhuja Avalokiteshvara
Western Tibet, 14th century
ground mineral pigment on cotton

Page 258
Arhat Dharmata and Direction Kings,
detail
Central Tibet, 19th century
ground mineral pigment on cotton

Page 259
Parvati
Northern India, 10th century
metal, silver inlay

Page 260
Arhat Vajriputra
Tibet, 18th century
ground mineral pigment on cotton

Page 261
Chakrasamvara
Eastern Tibet, 18th century
ground mineral pigment, fine gold line
on cotton

Page 262
Ganapati (Ganesha)
Tibet, 17th century
metal, gold inlay, with coral, turquoise,
and ruby insets

Page 263
Arhat Rahula
Tibet, 18th century
ground mineral pigment on cotton

Page 265
Black Garuda
Tibet, 18th century
ground mineral pigment on cotton

Page 268
Ngawang Lobsang Gyatso, 5th Dalai
Lama
Tibet, 17th century
ground mineral pigment, fine gold
line, red background on cotton

Page 271
Dudul Dorje, 13th Karmapa
Tibet, 18th century
ground mineral pigment on cotton

Page 272
Buddha Shakyamuni, detail
Tibet, 17th century

ground mineral pigment on cotton

Page 275
Maitreya
Mongolia, 19th century
bronze

Page 276
Buddha Ratnasambhava
Tibet, 14th century
ground mineral pigment on cotton

Page 277
Padmasambhava
Tibet, 18th century
ground mineral pigment on cotton

Page 279
Arhats Gopaka and Angaja
Tibet, 16th century
ground mineral pigment, fine gold line
on cotton

Page 280
Padmasambhava
Tibet, 19th century
ground mineral pigment on cotton

Page 282
Jetsun Dragpa Gyaltsen, detail

Central Tibet, 18th century
ground mineral pigment on cotton

Page 283
Buddha Shakyamuni
China, 18th century
ground mineral pigment on silk

Page 286
Arhat Angaja
Western Tibet, 17th century
ground mineral pigment on cotton

Page 289
Arhat Ajita
Eastern Tibet, 18th century
ground mineral pigment on cotton

Page 290
Arhat Vanavasin
Central Tibet, 16th century
ground mineral pigment, fine gold line
on cotton

Page 293
Arhat Kalika, detail
China, 19th century
ground mineral pigment on cotton

Page 294

Arhat Kanakavatsa
Tibet, 18th century
ground mineral pigment on cotton

Page 297
Arhat Kanaka Bharadvaja
Tibet, 19th century
ground mineral pigment on cotton

Page 299
Arhat Bakula
China, 17th century
textile

Page 300
Arhat Rahula
Tibet, 19th century
ground mineral pigment on cotton

Page 303
Arhat Chudapantaka
Eastern Tibet, 15th century
ground mineral pigment, fine gold line
on cotton

Page 304
Arhat Pindola Bharadvaja
Tibet, 17th century
ground mineral pigment, fine gold line
on cotton

Page 307
Arhat Pantaka
China, 17th century
ground mineral pigment on silk

Page 308
Arhat Gopaka
Tibet, 17th century
ground mineral pigment, fine gold line
on cotton

Page 320
Arhat Abheda
Tibet, 16th century
ground mineral pigment on cotton

Editor: Aiah Rachel Wieder
Art Director: Michelle Ishay
Designer: Laura Klynstra
Production Manager: Anet Sirna-Bruder

Cataloging-in-Publication Data has been applied for and may be
obtained from the Library of Congress.
ISBN: 978-0-8109-7295-7

Illustrations copyright © 2008 Rubin Museum of Art

Printed and bound in China

10 9 8 7 6 5 4 3 2 1

HNA ▌▌▌▌▌
harry n. abrams, inc.
a subsidiary of La Martinière Groupe
115 West 18th Street, New York, NY 10011
www.hnabooks.com